Easy Blues Piano

For Beginners

Southern House Publishing

tylermusic.co.uk

ISBN: 978-1-9997478-4-8

CONTENTS

Introduction

I assume that if you are reading this then you have an interest in learning to play the blues on piano, so I'll start by congratulating you on your fantastic taste in music. I like a fairly varied range of musical styles, but the blues is without doubt my favorite, it's what I enjoy listening to and playing the most, and no matter what I do play, I always seem to put an element of the blues in there somewhere.

The blues itself has been around for many years, originating from America with early recordings appearing in the 1920's, although the term 'blues' itself is fairly vague as there are quite a few different styles that developed at different times and in different regions, but they all share a lot of common ground.

The purpose of this book is to give the beginning blues piano player a first step into the style. Its aim is to cover the basics and get you started, the examples begin easy and then gradually increase in difficulty while introducing a few extra elements along the way. Once you have the basics that this book provides, you'll be at a point to then progress further with other publications of a higher difficulty level, or by using some of the sheet music that's available and hopefully from listening to the music too.

Thanks for reading this little intro, I hope you will find this book helpful on the start of your musical journey, but most of all just enjoy the blues, it's what music was made for.

The 12-Bar Blues

The blues traditionally consists of a repeated pattern of 12 bars, hence the term 12-bar blues. The varying chords used within the 12 bars creates what is termed a chord progression, being a progression of chords. In its most basic form this chord progression consists of only 3 chords, which makes it fairly easy to remember.

The three chords used in the blues are commonly referred to as being the ONE – FOUR – FIVE chords. This is more simply and commonly written as the roman numerals I – IV – V.

A Typical 12-Bar Blues Progression

Just a brief explanation here, we won't delve too deeply into this as we will use the specific chords throughout the book, as in 'C' or 'F' etc, but for reference this is how numerals work regarding chords. Shown below is the 'C' major scale, you can see that each note has been numbered which increases with each degree of the scale. So from here you can work out which chord the numeral refers to.

1. equals the 'C' chord
2. equals the 'D' chord
3. equals the 'E' chord
4. equals the 'F' chord
5. equals the 'G' chord
6. equals the 'A' chord
7. equals the 'B' chord

The 'C' Major Scale

So armed with this information, we can work out that for the key of 'C' the I – IV – V chords will be... C – F – G. Below is an example of a fairly typical but basic 12-bar blues chord progression in the key of 'C' that uses these three chords.

I   equals the 'C' chord
IV equals the 'F' chord
V   equals the 'G' chord

As you can see, there are four bars of 'C' which changes to the 'F' for two bars and returns back to the 'C' for two more. At this point it moves to the 'G' chord, but only for one bar as it then drops down to the 'F' for one bar and then finally finishes back where it all began with two bars of 'C'.

Initially at least, that's all there is to it, not too hard to remember, although the trick to such styles of playing is that these have to become completely internalized and recalled/used without thought, but that comes with practice.

Although it is only twelve bars long and has but three chords it might help you to remember the chord progression by breaking it down into three smaller sections of four bars. Not only because smaller chunks are always easier, but also because the feel of the music does kind of have three separate acts to it within its twelve bars, in a sense at least.

1.

The first four bars are all the 'C' chord. In a sense they kind of set the scene and get things rolling, asking a question perhaps, or highlighting some problem or dilemma. A blues singer for example might say about how his baby had left him.

2.

The second four bars are 'F' and 'C' in equal measure. The 'F' is a little like an initial response to the first four bars question, before returning back to the 'C' chord. The same singer might now repeat about his baby definitely seems to have left him.

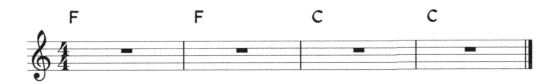

3.

The third four bars are different, the 'G' and the 'F' kind of resolve the question or dilemma, with the last two bars of 'C' then setting things up for the next twelve bars. The blues singer might now say about how she was mean to him, that he doesn't know what to do, or perhaps that he's actually better off without her, who knows.

Starting Out

The blues on a piano is perhaps different to some styles of music in that the two hands need to be independent, this is due to its improvisational nature and some of the timing you will encounter. Even at an early stage in your blues playing you should think about the left and right hands as being separate to each-other, as this will help you progress. With this in mind, it is advised to start practicing the left-hand first, as once you have this down it will take care of itself, allowing you greater freedom with your right-hand.

The first example is a simple bass-line consisting of just two notes (For the more theory minded among you, the root and third). Each is held for two beats, alternating between themselves throughout.

Practice this until it's pretty much committed to memory. Although the bass-line may be simple, you are also committing the blues chord progression to memory.

Here with have the same basic left-hand as the previous page, but this time it has been combined with a single note right-hand. There is nothing complicated here at this point, with all notes being from the 'C' major scale. Practice this to get used to combining the left-hand with the right-hand.

Although admittedly not very bluesy sounding, it's important to get used to playing through the changes (short for chord changes) of a blues progression before moving onto something a little more involved.

The Blues Notes

In order for the music to actually sound bluesy to some degree, we need to use different notes than just those that are found in the major scale. Blues music makes use of scales called the 'pentatonic' scales and also the 'blues' scales. These are a fairly involved subject to themselves, so to save complicating things, for the time being we will just take a look at perhaps the three most important notes. The numbers relate to the degrees of the major scale, which in this case is the 'C' major.

1.

First is the flattened 3rd. In the key of 'C' this is the 'E♭'.

2.

Next is the flattened 5th. In the key of 'C' this is the 'G♭'.

3.

Last is the flattened 7th (or dominant 7th as opposed to the major 7th). In the key of 'C' this is the 'B♭'.

These three notes all stem from the blues scale (key of 'C') and their use is important to give the music some of the 'blues sound'.

A Blue Note Blues

In this twelve bar example we have the same two note bass-line as before, but with the right-hand we introduce the three extra notes we mentioned earlier, the so called 'blue-notes'.

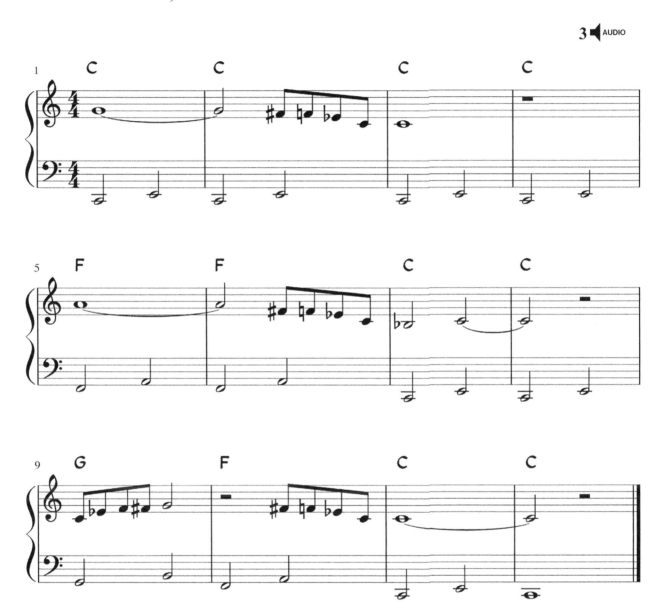

Three Note Bass-Line

Now it's time to add a little something to the left-hand bass-line by the addition of the 5th. In the key of 'C' this is the note 'G'.

This three note pattern has the root note for two counts and the 3rd and 5th for one count each.

Practice the left-hand separately to begin with over a twelve bar progression until you feel comfortable with it.

First Time Blues

This example consists of twenty-four bars, being two twelve bar sequences with one following the other. That is how a twelve bar blues song is created, the progression is repeated again and again. Although at a higher level this progression can be altered quite a lot.

First Time Blues continued....

Second 12 Bars

Walking Bass

We will progress now onto a four note pattern. Here each note is valued equally with the count of one beat. Although the timing is simpler than the previous one, it is slighter busier. This is a simple version of what might be termed a walking bass-line, although to begin with we aren't walking too far.

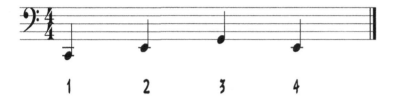

Try this left-hand pattern over a twelve bar progression. Practice until you are comfortable with it and then try playing 'Kitty Cat Blues'.

13

Kitty Cat Blues

First 12 Bars

Kitty Cat Blues continued...

Second 12 Bars

Triplets

The use of triplets is extremely common in blues piano. A triplet is where each individual beat is divided equally into three.

Shown below is a bar of triplets, note how each beat (there are four with the timing being in 4/4) is divided by three notes.

When considering the timing of these, it might help to think of it as each individual cluster of triplets having the ¾ timing of a waltz. As such you would count three beats 1 – 2 – 3. But instead of this count of three taking up the entire bar (as in ¾ timing) it is within the space of one beat instead.

Below you can see each of the four beats in the bar sharing the space of each group of triplets. Practice the timing as shown below. Use the count of 1 – 2 – 3 for the right-hand as you play the single bass notes.

8+9 ◀ AUDIO

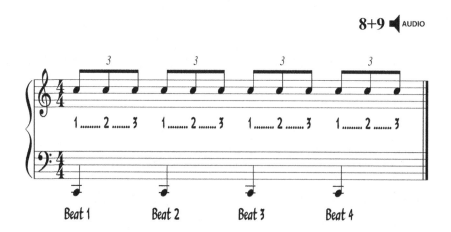

Triplets are often used in fast repetitive passages like the one below.

Bare in mind that although it might look very busy/complicated on the page, it's actually far simpler than it first appears.

The example below shows the same notes written as single beats, all you are doing is repeating the exact same thing three times per beat instead of once. When you think of it that way... it is far easier than the busy notation above makes it appear.

Practice playing repetitive triplets with the right hand over a twelve bar progression and then try playing 'Walking The Blues'.

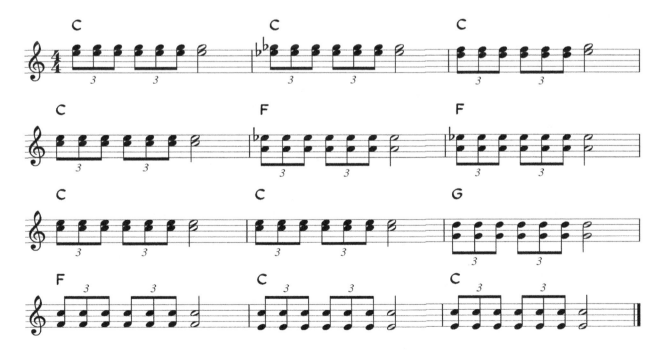

Walking The Blues

Walking The Blues continued...

Second 12 Bars

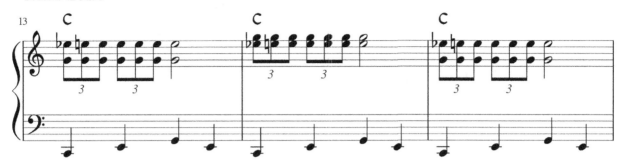

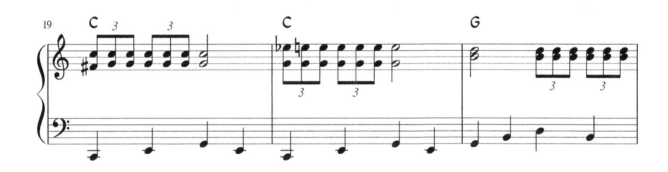

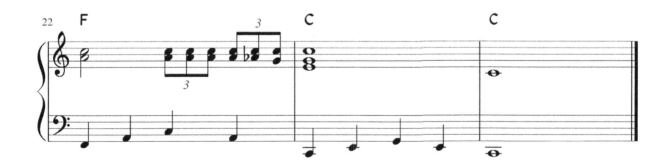

Repeating Triplet Patterns

Using triplets in small repeating patterns as shown below is a common practice in blues.

1.

2.

3.

Practice playing the repeating patterns of triplets before moving on to include the left-hand in 'Triple Blues'.

You will also come across triplet timing where instead of each triplet being a separate note, some of them are tied together. This can be written in two different ways, either with a tie sign between the notes.

1.

Or by using a note of different value for the triplets that are tied together.

2.

The timing is shown below. Nothing really changes here, except that there is now two counts for the longer of the two notes.

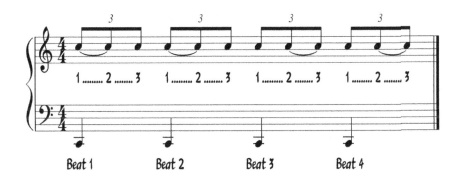

Triple-Blues

First 12 Bars

22

Triple-Blues continued...

Second 12 Bars

Walking Bass 2

The type of left-hand bass-line we have been looking at is commonly called the 'walking-bass', so called because it walks up and down the keyboard. But so far we haven't been walking very far, so here it's time we extended it slightly.

We are now moving through the scale from the root at the bottom, right through to the root an octave higher, before walking back down again.

Practice this over a twelve bar progression before playing 'Walking The Blues 2'. It is perhaps a little trickier as the fingering will require you to cross-over your thumb at the top.

Walking The Blues 2

Walking The Blues 2 continued...

Walking Bass 3

We can take this further again by including extra notes, here we are adding the 7th. Please note that this is the dominant 7th and not the major 7th. In the key of 'C' this is B♭.

Practice this over a twelve bar progression until you feel comfortable with it. It will require you to cross-over your thumb at the top. Then try playing 'Walking The Blues 3'.

14 ◀ AUDIO

Note that the 7th is not used on bars nine and ten in this instance. Walking bass-lines are normally varied throughout a song.

Walking The Blues 3

First 12 Bars

Walking The Blues 3 continued...

Syncopation

Syncopation simply refers to how music can be played in a way that includes notes and rhythms that are unexpected and off-beat. Off-beat meaning that they aren't directly in line with the main beats of the music.

Here you can see the right-hand notes all fall exactly on each beat. **On-beat**.

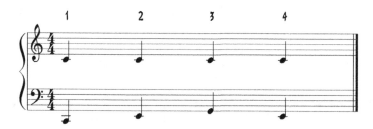

Here you can see that each right-hand note falls on the second half of each beat. **Off-beat**.

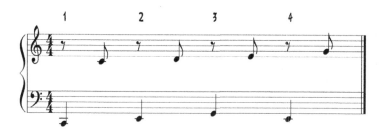

This can be found in many forms, often with the notes being tied over to the next beat and often into the next bar as shown below.

Jump The Blues

Here we have two different versions of the same thing, both highly syncopated. The first is played straight, with the second using triplets in the right-hand. You can hear the big difference this subtle change makes to the music.

Jump The Blues continued...

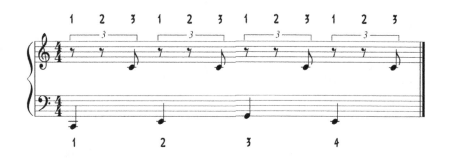

Second 12 Bars

Syncopation With Triplets

In the next example 'Walking The Dog Blues' notice the timing of the syncopated triplets with the anticipation of the tied triplets, plus the carry over into the next beat or the next bar.

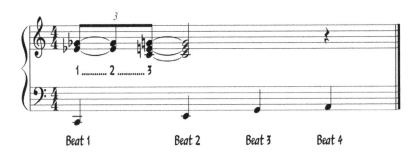

Often the same thing is used to tie into the next bar, which works nicely at chord changes.

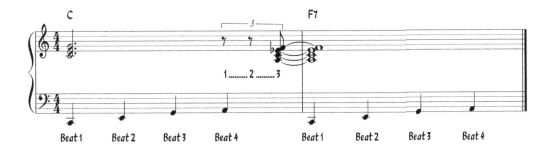

Remember the two ways of writing a triplet note that is tied within its own group.

Walking The Dog Blues

First 12 Bars

Walking The Dog Blues continued...

Second 12 Bars

Introducing Boogie-Blues

Blues and its off-shoot blues based boogie-woogie have a lot in common, and some blues piano is firmly based within this style using some of the same left-hand patterns.

The first left-hand pattern to learn is often referred to as the 'chop' or 'chopping bass'. There are quite a few variations but this is where it all starts.

To begin with we will simplify it slightly. This example consists of just two notes, each played simultaneously directly on each beat.

Try this left-hand pattern over twelve bars. Practice until you are comfortable, aiming for approximately between 100 and 120 bpm. Then try playing the 'First Boogie Blues'.

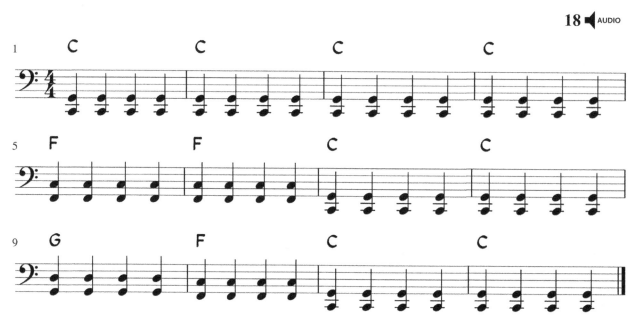

First Boogie Blues

First Boogie Blues continued...

Version 2

The next version is altered so that it includes the sixth every other beat. A subtle difference but it makes a large difference.

Try this left-hand pattern over a twelve bar progression. Practice until you are comfortable with it, aiming to go up to between 100 and 120 bpm, then try playing 'Up 'n' Down Blues'.

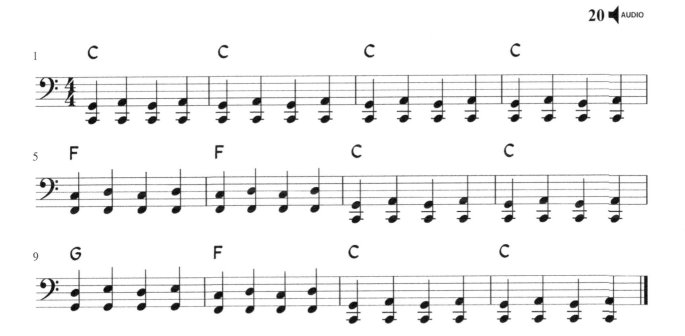

Up 'n' Down Blues

Up 'n' Down Blues continued.....

Version 3

Moving on from here we keep the same basic pattern, but we change to quavers or half beats and double up on the frequency, now playing it twice per beat.

This pattern is found in blues, boogie-woogie and rock'n'roll. It's simple and repetitive, making it easy to remember, but it takes time and practice to absorb fully to the point where it can be played without thought through the changes. Keeping the timing tight and consistent is the key to playing it well.

Try this left-hand pattern over twelve bars. Practice until you are comfortable with it, aiming to get up to between 100 and 120bpm, then try playing 'Straight Blues'.

22 AUDIO

42

Straight Blues

First 12 Bars

Straight Blues continued...

Second 12 Bars

The Triplet Feel

Now it's time to change things again by introducing a triplet or swing feel to the music. This is generally how blues music is played so it is important to get the feel of this down.

Strangely it can be seen written in notation in a number of ways, we must cover them all so that you will understand the sheet music that you might possibly encounter in the future, but for now we will begin by showing it in a technically correct manner.

This is the common 'chopping' type bass-line that we had begun to look at, only here it is written as it is usually played, with a triplet feel.

The pattern is essentially the same as the previous one, but now it consists of a long note and a short note. This make a large change to the feel of the music, creating the triplet type shuffle feel that we mentioned.

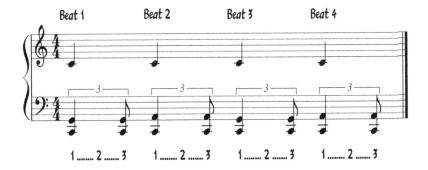

Each beat is split into three for the triplets. The first longer notes have a count of two, with the second shorter notes the count of one.

Blues Shuffle Bass-Line

This is the full version of the 'chopping bass' as it is usually played. Try this pattern over a twelve bar progression, practicing until you are comfortable with the triplet/shuffle feel, aiming for between 100 and 120bpm. If you are unsure of the sound/feel this should have, then listen to the audio example or a suitable blues/boogie-woogie record. Listening to blues music is a very important aspect of learning anyway and I'd encourage you to do so as much as possible. Incidentally, just to clarify, the triplet feel in blues piano is often referred to as being a shuffle or blues shuffle, but it all means the same thing.

Notation Version 1

An important point to make is that this type left-hand never seems to be written using triplets in sheet music. This is probably due to the extra work of notating the triplets all the time, plus the fact that it makes the page look very busy and overly complicated.

In reality the triplet feel tends to be written in two different ways that imply the triplet feel, rather than notate it correctly. This might sound strange but it's simple enough, and now that you have already practiced the triplet feel and understand how it sounds there is nothing to worry about.

One method uses dotted-quavers and semi-quavers. This come close to the true timing and does a nice job of implying the timing, but would sound odd if played exactly as it is written. But that's fine, as you already know how it should sound, this is merely reminding you of the required feel.

Below shows you the implied timing, rather than the timing the notation actually shows.

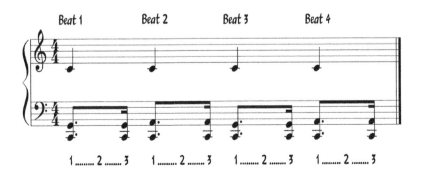

Try this left-hand pattern again over a twelve bar progression, but this time looking at it notated using the dotted-quavers and semi-quavers. Remember, don't play it exactly as shown, as it's meant to be played with a triplet feel, counting 1 – 2 – 3 over each beat. The notation is merely implying the feel. When you are comfortable with the idea, try adding the right-hand by playing 'Shuffle Boogie Blues'.

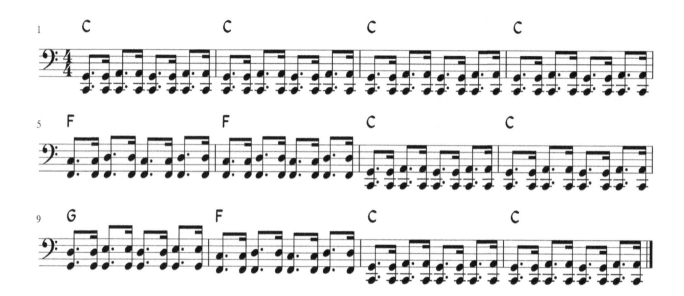

Shuffle Boogie Blues

First 12 Bars

49

Shuffle Boogie Blues continued...

Right-Hand Triplets

Because the left-hand is now using a triplet feel, this actually makes it far easier to play triplets over the top with the right-hand, as the timing now flows together rather than contrasting. Although contrasting rhythms can be used to great effect at times and creates interest.

You can see how the timing of the notes in both the left-hand and right-hand now coincide with each-other. The first two notes of the right-hand inhabit the same time as the first note of the left-hand, with the third and last triplet coinciding with the last note of the left-hand.

Shown here with the left-hand in triplets.

Shown here as you might find it written, yes it's not technically correct but don't look at me, I don't make up the rules.

Triple Blues Shuffle

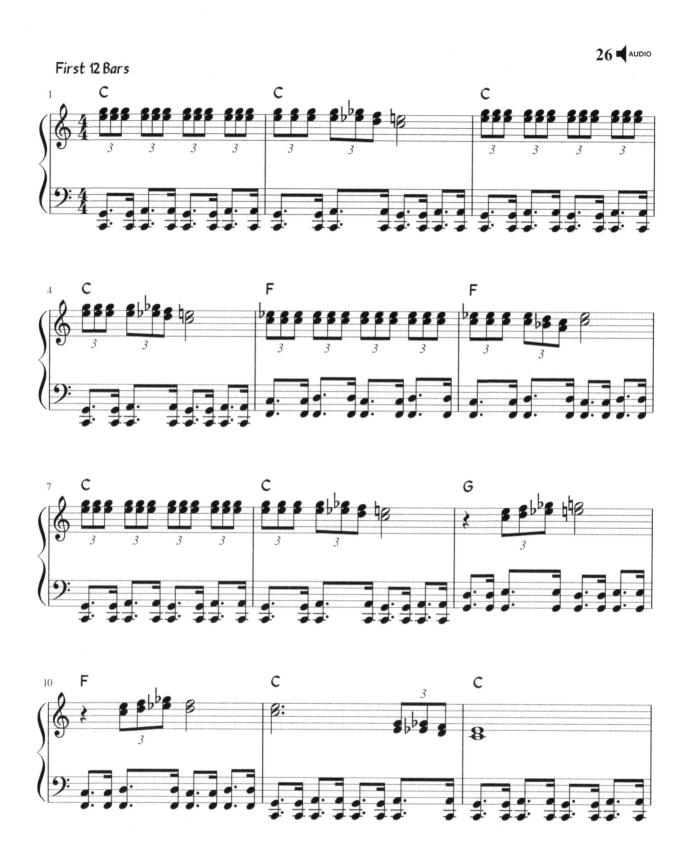

Triple Blues Shuffle continued...

Second 12 Bars

Notation Version 2

I mentioned previously that there are two ways in that the triplet feel is notated, rather than the technically correct way of using actual triplets. So it's time to look at the other way, as this seems to increasingly be the preferred method in blues sheet music these days.

Yes, as you may have noticed it is shown as being straight quavers, written just as it was when we first looked at the 'chop' pattern with straight timing.

Confused? Well I wouldn't blame you, but don't worry as once you know the triplet feel you should be playing (and fortunately we have already covered it) there is no need to have it notated correctly, all you need are the notes.

When music with a triplet/swing feel is notated like this, it is accompanied by a sign at the beginning of the sheet music (normally only the first page) to tell you that it is in fact played with a triplet feel. Otherwise, you'd never know.

Below is a typical symbol used to state that the piece is to be played with a triplet feel, although it's normally a bit smaller than this one.

So just to clarify this further, the first quaver of a beat is worth the count of two triplets. The second quaver is worth the count of one triplet.

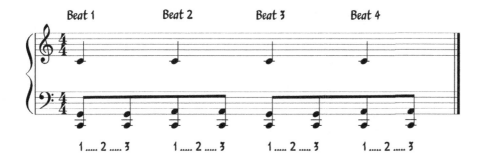

Shown again to include the right-hand, which obviously also uses the same notation method.

The exception to this rule is of course when all three triplets are to be played, this still has to be written the correct way.

I can imagine that if this is new to you, then having different ways of writing the same thing may seem a little confusing, but now that you are aware of it you won't be confused when you look at the blues sheet music that is available out there.

Play this pattern again over a twelve bar progression, but this time looking at it notated with straight quavers. Once you feel comfortable with the idea of this, move on and try playing 'Triple Feel Blues'.

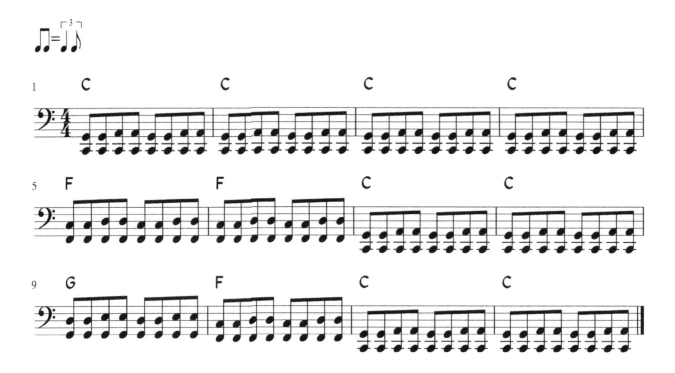

It might seem strange playing something that is actually different to what is written, but it has become the common way of writing blues music. So I want you to become accustomed to it now, as it will then help you a lot when you advance further.

Triple Feel Blues

Triple Feel Blues continued...

The next example piece changes the chord progression slightly. Here the second bar is now the 'IV' chord. This is probably more commonly used than the 'I' chord.

Another change is the left-hand bass-line now moves up further to include the use of the dominant 7th. This extra note isn't used consistently on every single bar, keeping things changing adds a degree of interest to the music.

Practice this left-hand pattern over a twelve bar progression, aiming between 100 and 120bpm, then try playing 'Seventh Blues'.

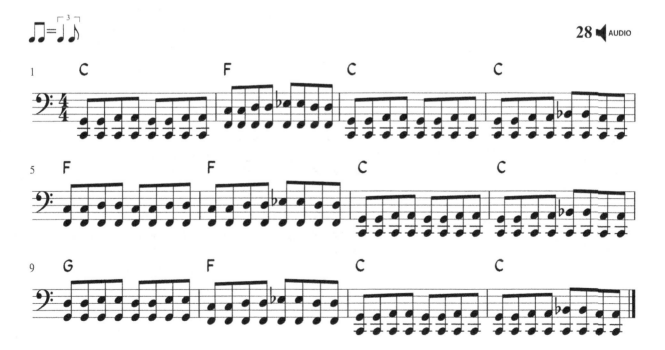

59

Seventh Blues

Seventh Blues continued...

Second 12 Bars

Beginning New Orleans

New Orleans blues is a bit of a style to itself, although having much in common with the blues music that developed in other regions, it is quite distinctive. It has a strong Latin influence, often using a Rumba type beat which is where it differs mainly from other styles.

There are many complex left-hand patterns out there, but starting out for the first time we will look at this three note example that will get you used to the highly syncopated nature of this style of music.

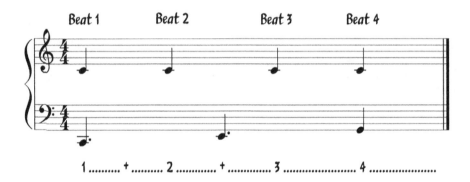

The first two notes are dotted crotchets, both worth 1½ beats each, with the last note being a crotchet worth 1 beat. You could try practicing it to a metronome to help keep it tight, and/or play each of the beats with the right-hand (as in the example) to get the timing against.

If you find it tricky, look at this way. Playing the four notes on the beat with the right-hand, the first bass note starts exactly with the right-hand on beat one. Then play the right-hand beat two note, the second bass note is half a beat after that one. Then the last bass note falls exactly on beat four, so it's only the middle bass note that is out of place, off-beat.

When you have the timing sorted, try practicing it over a twelve bar progression until you feel comfortable with it. Try working these up to around 120 bpm.

31 ◀ AUDIO

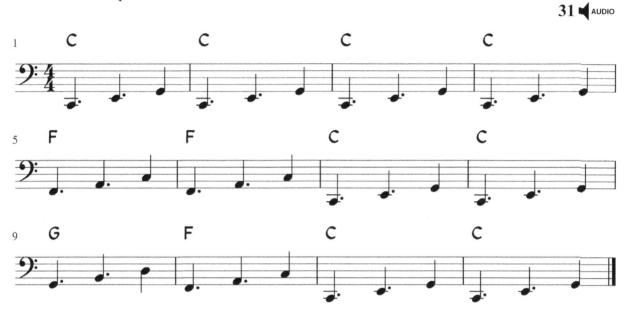

This is also often played with octaves, so if you feel comfortable, why not give that a go as well, or come back to it later on. Bare in mind that if you have smaller hands, then this might not be ideal for you.

32 ◀ AUDIO

Once you are happy with this bass-line, try practicing it with the right-hand. Here the right-hand is just playing chords on the beat, which will help get used to the syncopated feel. Once you are comfortable with it, move on to 'First Nola Blues'. Nola is short for New Orleans.

First Nola Blues

First Nola Blues continued...

Second 12 Bars

66

Practice Suggestions

Practice Time

I will state the obvious and say that to progress and improve at anything you need to spend time doing that thing. So needless to say that the more time you spend on the piano the better you will get. But I will say one thing, consistency is the key. The best way to progress is to practice everyday, this keeps everything fresh in your mind and will really help push you forward. And when I say everyday, it doesn't necessarily mean hours and hours (although if you can then great, the more the merrier) but just put in whatever you can spare, even ten minutes if that's all you have, the main thing is to keep it regular without large gaps in-between.

Metronome

Using a metronome while practicing is highly recommended. The use of one will really help with keeping the timing tight throughout and also when learning a part that has timing you are unaccustomed to. When I say metronome, use whatever you have, which may literally be a mechanical metronome or one on an electric instrument or even an app on your phone. Playing along to a drum backing is also an option, and there are a few drum tracks available to download, although these are of course at set tempos.

Listen To The Music

To really get the feel of the blues it is vital that you listen to it as much as possible. This really helps you internalize the sound, which in turn will help enable you to recreate it on the piano. There is a short list of possible starting points on the suggested listening page, just in-case you're not sure where to start.

Suggested Listening

Without doubt one of the most important things you can do when learning a style of music is to listen to it, and I mean a lot. This may sound obvious, but you really want to make a point of listening to the music that you are trying to play. While you can learn songs merely from reading sheet music, the dots and dashes really don't convey the feeling of the music the same way and the brain absorbs the sounds that you hear, which makes it far easier to then translate that sound onto the piano.

While the piano can be heard on many blues albums over the years, for the sake of learning the piano I would suggest that you highlight albums that are either solo piano (quite rare) or at least spotlight the piano rather than being just a small part in the background of a band. With that in mind, here are a few suggestions from my own collection to get started with.

Dr John Plays Mac Rebennack: The Legendary Sessions Vol. 1

Dr John Plays Mac Rebennack: The Legendary Sessions Vol. 2

James Booker: Spider On The Keys

Johnnie Johnson: Johnnie B. Bad

Otis Spann: Is The Blues

Otis Spann: Walking The Blues

Pinetop Perkins: After Hours

Pinetop Perkins: The Complete Hightone Sessions

Downloadable Audio

Audio files based on the examples within the book are available to download from the website in MP3 format, simply follow the instructions below.

To access and download the MP3 audio files, simply visit the website...

www.tylermusic.co.uk

- Go to newsletter page
- Enter email address
- Receive return email (please check spam/junk folders)
- Click on link within email
- Select relevant book title
- Enter the password... **easyblues848**

Once downloaded please save them for future use.

The email address is used only for this purpose and the very occasional news of publications and blues and boogie-woogie events.

Downloadable Audio Files

1) Left-Hand 1
2) Left + Right-Hand 1
3) Blue Note Blues
4) Three Note Bass-Line
5) First Time Blues
6) Walking-Bass LH 1
7) Kitty Cat Blues
8) Triplet Timing Slow
9) Triplet Timing Fast
10) Walking The Blues
11) Triple Blues
12) Walking-Bass LH 2
13) Walking The Blues 2
14) Walking-Bass LH 3
15) Walking The Blues 3
16) Jump The Blues
17) Walking The Dog Blues

18) Boogie LH 1
19) First Boogie Blues
20) Boogie LH 2
21) Up 'n' Down Blues
22) Boogie LH 3
23) Straight Blues
24) Boogie LH Shuffle
25) Shuffle Boogie Blues
26) Triple Blues Shuffle
27) Triple Feel Blues
28) Boogie LH 4
29) Seventh Blues
30) Nola Timing
31) Nola Bass-Line 1
32) Nola Bass-Line 2
33) Nola LH + RH
34) First Nola Blues

The Complete-Blues Piano

Want to learn more blues piano...

The complete blues piano is a comprehensive guide to playing and improvising blues piano. It covers the fundamental principles of the blues and includes in-depth theory and techniques, along with example blues pieces to learn/study along with downloadable audio. Ranging from fast boogie-type blues to slow blues, Chicago through to New Orleans, beginners to intermediate, this has it covered. 240 pages.

Start playing authentic blues today

Also Available

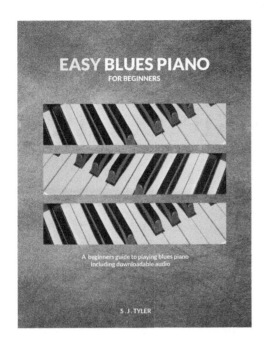

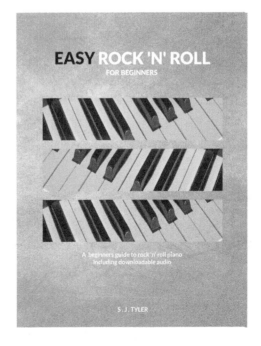

Tyler music.co.uk

For further piano books, sheet music and information on blues
and boogie woogie music and events
visit the website at...

www.tylermusic.co.uk

Made in the USA
Middletown, DE
13 June 2021